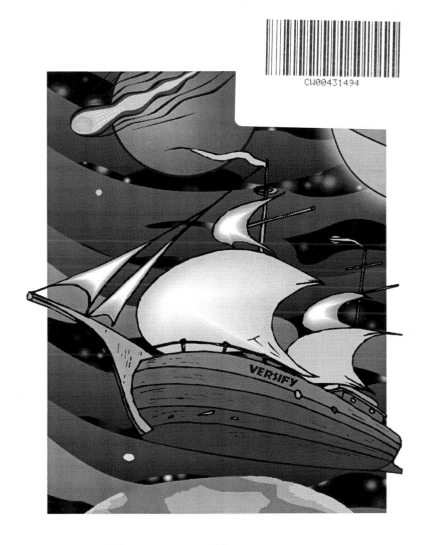

POETIC VOYAGES
LANARKSHIRE

Edited by Dave Thomas

First published in Great Britain in 2001 by
YOUNG WRITERS
Remus House,
Coltsfoot Drive,
Peterborough, PE2 9JX
Telephone (01733) 890066

HB ISBN 0 75433 122 9
SB ISBN 0 75433 123 7

FOREWORD

Young Writers was established in 1991 with the aim to promote creative writing in children, to make reading and writing poetry fun.

This year once again, proved to be a tremendous success with over 88,000 entries received nationwide.

The Poetic Voyages competition has shown us the high standard of work and effort that children are capable of today. It is a reflection of the teaching skills in schools, the enthusiasm and creativity they have injected into their pupils shines clearly within this anthology.

The task of selecting poems was therefore a difficult one but nevertheless, an enjoyable experience. We hope you are as pleased with the final selection in *Poetic Voyages Lanarkshire* as we are.

CONTENTS

Melanie McKinlay	57
Lisa Sommerville	57
Sarah-Jane Hunter	58
Stephen Stewart	58
Sean Gilfillan	59
Laura Millar	59
Ross Jack	60
Nick McCaskie	60
Craig Stenhouse	60
Shona Johnston	61
Ailsa Anderson	61
Aiden Rogers	61
David Hamilton	62
Tom Melvin	62
Laura Kirland	63
Caroline Wilson	63
Asten Hill	64
Andrew Payne	64
Jenna Browning	65
Andrew Leckenby	65
Ashleigh Brown	66
Alix Reid	66
Gillian Haddow	66
Andrew Murray	67

Noble Primary School

Aimee Raeside	68
Ashleigh Aitchison	68
Hannah Callander	69
Emma Blue	69
Shanon Cook	70
Danielle Mullen	70
Vivian Miller	70
Andrew Lennox	71
Jordan Ferguson	71
Heather McAlpine	72
Jordan Meharry	72

Kirsty Lawrie	73
Kirstin Tait	73
Kris McArthur	74
Gary Wilson	74
Jamie N Kelly	74
Susan McRae	75

Old Monkland Primary School

Lauren Lynn	75
Jenna Swan	76
Stephanie Woods	76
Amy Calderwood	77
Ashley Stewart	77
Ross Richardson	78
Adam Skinner	78
Scott Ward	79
Nicola Brady	79

Plains Primary School

Heather Baillie	80
Jamie Martin	80
Cheryl MacDonald	81
Chris Arbuckle	81
Jamie Meechan	82
Andrew Gibb	82
Gael White	83
Scott Mitchell	83
Stuart MacFarlane	84
Stephenie Condron	84

Robert Smillie Memorial Primary School

Harry Hamilton	85
Emma Thomson	85
Mark Douglas	85
Stephanie Hammel	86
Lisa Hamilton	86
Gemma Craw	86

Rachelle Waugh	87
Russell Pate	87
Kayleigh Hamilton	88
William McIlvaney	88
Gary Houston	89

St Aidan's Primary School

Louise McCulloch	89
Jennifer Lynch	90
Jack Friskey	90
Marta Zadruzynska	91
Louise McLean	91
Andrew Ashe	92
James Bradley	92
Melissa Clare	93
Alison Fulton	93
Ciara Donnelly	94
David Welsh	94
Jonathan Dalziel	95
Carla Leith	96
Monica Donnelly	96
Emma Hepburn	97
Amy Sloan	98
Marc Montgomery	98
Gemma Fulton	99
Andrew Welsh	99

St Mary's Primary School

Andrew Barton	100
Emma Jane McCulloch	100
Rachel McKinnon	101
Kevin Carr	102
Santino Palazzo	102
David Breakey	103
Sean Gustinelli	104
Katie O'Hanlon	104
Elisha-Jane Burns	105

The Poems

MY BEST FRIEND

My best friend is really fun,
In the summer we play in the sun.
My best friend is really cool,
If I hated her I'd be a fool!

My best friend I can talk to,
Everything we say is all true.
My best friend is someone I can trust
To keep my secrets is a must.

My best friend I really like
She even lets me go on her bike.
My best friend lets me stay the night
And when I do we never fight.

My best friend shares with me
When she does I shine with glee
My best friend is really kind
And If I borrow she doesn't mind.

My best friend is really nice,
If she has chocolate she gives me a slice.
My best friend is the best,
She is better than the rest!

Jill Robley (11)
Braidwood Primary School

ENERGY

Light, heat, movement and sound
All types of energy can be found
In everything that we do
And it all starts off with you!

First you move about the room
Everyone watching as you zoom
In that time you're creating power
Sound and movement to last you an hour.

Solar energy comes from the sun
Our teacher showed us it can be fun
To make the fan go round and round
And the buzzer to make a sound.

Then we went to Hunterston Power Station
Where they told us they supply electricity to the whole nation
We were also told that coal comes from under the soil,
And the water that comes from the sea they also boil!

At the end of our energy topic
It definitely wasn't microscopic.
We have learnt so much, I'm quite amazed!
I give 'energy' my full praise.

Amy Ramage (11)
Braidwood Primary School

ENERGY

Energy produces light
So that you can see at night
Energy has a form
That will keep you nice and warm

A new energy is solar power
We use it by the hour
We use it at work and home
They even use it at the Millennium Dome

Wind is another source
But we all know of that of course
The windmills have to go round
That is where the energy is found

As the tide moves in and out
It leaves lots of energy about
In the sky or on the ground
Lots of energy can be found

On my front cover I have a picture of the sun
The energy topic has been fun
I know now when I go to bed at night
The importance of turning off the light.

Kirsty Lake (11)
Braidwood Primary School

CHRISTMAS IS

The lights are on the Christmas tree,
The carollers are singing, full of glee.
How many presents will Santa Clause bring,
I think I can hear his sleigh bells ring.

Rudolph's nose is guiding the way,
For Santa to come this Christmas day.
For boys and girls who have been good this year,
There will be a stocking full of cheer.

Now Christmas Day at last has come,
My Advent calendar is all done
But Christmas lunch is at one,
With turkey and pudding and lots of fun.

After lunch we go out to play,
Whizzing down the hill on our sleigh.
Christmas Day is full of cheer
The best bit is we do it all next year.

Ryan Haynes (10)
Braidwood Primary School

ENERGY

Energy was our science topic
Neutrons and atoms are microscopic
The forms of energy that we found
Were heat, light and obviously sound

Some sources of energy are wind, wave and sun
To do the topic again would not be fun
The topic seemed to last for ages
Our topics include over thirty-five pages

When we went to Hunterston B
We saw the bubble in the sea
As I walked to the building with my class
We saw the rabbits in the grass

When we visited the power station
The guides gave us useful information
The sources of energy wind, wave and sun
Will be around for years to come.

Roslyn Lake (11)
Braidwood Primary School

MY BEST FRIENDS

My best friends are the twins,
They even sometimes go in a spin.
We like football and tennis galore,
So I always knock on the door.

We like to play basketball,
Their hoop is attached to their garage wall,
We like to score,
But we like chocolate more.

We play at the park,
Until it's dark,
We read some books,
And we like to cook.

Roslyn and Kirsty play in their paddling pool,
We even think school is quite cool.
Mrs Black is our favourite teacher,
We even try hard to please her.

Stephanie Howieson (11)
Braidwood Primary School

FRIENDSHIP MEANS . . .

Friends are the best
They're simply better than the rest,
Once you've got them, they're always there
Being kind, considerate and fair.
When you're sad you cannot deny
They'll cheer you up before you cry.

Friends are the best of all,
They'll never let you fall
Some are playful, some are funny
But the smiles on their faces are always sunny.
With their eyes shining like a star
They are always near, never far.

When you're happy sing a song
They'll most likely sing along.
When you're playing 'tag' by the garden tree
Who'll go hey maybe you or me?
We'll play together for hours in the sun
Laughing and sharing in lots of fun.

So please be thankful for the friends you've got
They're surely the best of the lot!

Catherine Bryce (11)
Braidwood Primary School

RUGBY

Rugby is dangerous,
Rugby is fun,
I play it because
I can run.

I have played for many years,
Four years in fact,
And only once have they shouted,
'Bring that stretcher over here
To this young lad.'

I always dream of the day,
When I will walk onto that Murrayfield turf
To play for Scotland.

I will run past them all
And score a try -
To remember the day
I walked onto that great pitch.

I remember the days when rugby
Was nothing to me,
But in the future I can see me
Walking on for Scotland.

John Stewart (10)
Carmichael Primary School

MUM'S COOKING

As I come home from school
Smelling the sweet aroma,
I say to myself, 'She's cooking!'
I think of a chocolate cake,
All creamy and brown
Or a pie all crispy and crumbly;
But as I go through the door
It's just a brown crusty loaf
All tender after baking.
So I trudge in after a day's working,
And Mum guesses what I'm thinking.
She gives me a slice and I just nibble it;
So she goes to the fridge and opens it wide
And takes out the biggest, best, widest chocolate cake
I have ever seen.
I take a slice and eat it carefully -
And then I taste the b-e-a-u-t-i-f-u-l creamy chocolate
As it melts on my tongue.

Emma Bone (11)
Carmichael Primary School

MY BEDROOM

Ma bedroom is an awfu' mess
The bed is in the middle
The duvet hinging aff a bit
A dinnae really care.

Ma bedroom is an awfu' mess
Nothing can you find.
I try to look fur ma claes
Bit God knows where they are.

Ma mammy says it's needin'
A wee-redd-up.
A tell her a cudnae care
Bit at the end o' the day
Ma mammy gives up
And a mess ma bedroom stays!

John Brown (9)
Carmichael Primary School

MY BIG BROTHER

My big brother fights me all the time.
He pushes me into walls
And shoves me into chairs.
He gets me on the ground
And tickles me to death;
He would do anything to annoy me
And he does!
But he's my brother and I guess it's all right
Because it doesn't hurt.
He makes very funny jokes
That make me laugh until it hurts.
He pretends he is nice to Mum
But he actually is a bit wicked!
He will be nice at times,
But then strange another.
He is stronger than me
So he always wins at our little fights,
But that's my big brother for you -
And I wouldn't change him for the world.

Graham Veale (10)
Carmichael Primary School

MY PEST OF A BROTHER

He messes up my room
And switches my telly on and off.
Mucks up the PlayStation
Gets me into trouble.
Breaks my toys,
And hits me with his plastic golf clubs
On the head.
He comes in my room at night
When I'm trying to sleep,
He spills my breakfast
On the floor.
He runs away with my school sweatshirt
Then I trip him up!
In winter he pushes his pedal tractor
Into the snowman I make.
At Christmas he throws the paper in my room.
Then I tidy it up
The best thing about my brother
Is when he gets food for me!

Christopher Nicholl (10)
Carmichael Primary School

MY FAVOURITE THING

I like to play snooker,
I like to play badminton.
I like to play my Game Boy,
But most of all I like to play football.

I play football every day,
In my back garden.
I pretend I am Davie Cooper,
The greatest player ever.
I pretend I play for Scotland in the World Cup.

When I watch it on telly,
I shout and cheer so loud.
My mum says I am blaring,
But I keep cheering so loud!

Andrew Clarkson (10)
Carmichael Primary School

MY LITTLE SISTER

Every morning she runs to my room
And hits me on the face,
I get dressed
Put my shoes on
But she undoes my shoelace.

I go downstairs to watch TV
While she plays with toys,
But I can't hear it because
She makes too much noise.

When I go to bed
She steals my ted
And I have to get it back.

She goes into my room
And takes my hamster
Out of its cage.
She drops it and loses it
And my mum goes into a rage!

I can't wait till she is older
So I can get some peace.

Melissa Kennedy (10)
Carmichael Primary School

THE WRESTLING BOOK

When I was nine
I read a lot.
I read Roald Dahl, Michael Bond
And lots more.
But I loved, and I mean loved,
To read wrestling things.
I love wrestling like
Jeff Hardy, Rock
And Stone Cold.
But one day my mum saw me reading it
And grabbed it from me
And I said, 'Gi'me it back!'
Mum said, 'No, no you're not reading this violence!'
And I was grounded for a week
And I hated her for that.

Michael Ferguson (10)
Carmichael Primary School

BOOKS

Stand up,
Walk to the shelf,
Grab several million books,
Sit down
And . . .
Begin to read.
(wait for it)
Delve into Darwin,
Clatter into Kipling,
Tear into Terry Deary,
Merge with myths,
Fantasy with fiction
Fun with fact.
That's a book!

Laura May (11)
Carmichael Primary School

DOGS

There are black dogs,
White dogs and poodles, pink and fluffy.
They leave hairs almost everywhere,
If they're big, small or puppies;
There are big dogs with bones
Roly dogs that spray all over with water,
Fat dogs that eat all the time;
There are thin dogs, skinny and bony,
Then there are fighting dogs and working dogs
With muscles huge and round.
There are dogs that swim and jump and play
And gallop all around each day;
They itch and scratch and lick themselves
And some just sleep all day.

Francis Derrington (9)
Carmichael Primary School

A BIRD'S JOURNEY

Swooshing up and down I can see the waves crashing against the shore
The sound of birds singing in the sound of those waves
And the strong wind pushing against my bright yellow beak

There is the salt smell from the dark, blue sea
The top of the mountains covered in thick white snow
And sheep shaking their fluffy coats in the swirling wind

I hear the sound of the wind in my frail small ears . . .
It's wonderful when you are as free as a bird.

Lyle Scougall (10)
Carnbroe Primary School

THE SPIRIT OF THE SEA

I am the spirit of the sea
I go where the sea glistens like diamonds
I live where the sea looks black
Black as the sky at night
I am lonely
Lonely as the hermit crab in his shell
I venture to the reefs and am careful not to make a sound
I don't want to startle the fish with my ghostly appearance
I float around a sleeping whale
And go to my cave till morning

I hear the whales singing
It is as beautiful as wind chimes in a soft breeze in summer
I still remember my own life before this
It was as dull and glum as it is now
No one knows how I feel
Sad and miserable like I was not meant to be born
The whale's song haunts me as it has done before

The fish swim in silver clusters
I go through them but they don't feel me
Just a coldness, a strange coldness
Too miserable to notice anything
I am just too sad
No one knows me, no one likes me, no one sees me.

I hate the salty smell of the sea
The angry crash of the waves
The underwater currents that blow me away
The sharks that chase me for fun
If I had one wish, just one
I know what it would be.

Fiona McDonald (10)
Carnbroe Primary School

A DARK JOURNEY

We start the engine
It chugs away
We're going to war
We're going today

I look at the sail
It's magnificent and white
It could light up the ship
On the darkest night

The waves are crashing
Against the vessel
The sound is rare
And very special

We're going to kill
That's bad enough
But this mission is long
And its going to be tough

I can feel the sadness
And the fear
In the ship's
atmosphere

We're on a voyage
With allies good
To keep the world
The way it should.

Ross Cowan (10)
Carnbroe Primary School

THE WRECK

There she lies
The rotted ship, away from human vanity
Like a palace without a king or queen

I swim
into the captain's cabin
his hat hangs upon the wall tired and worn out

I swim out flicking from wall to wall
All the way to the ballroom
I sometimes hear people dancing and laughing
But now it's just broken glass all over the place.

I swam out to a narrowed corridor
I stared sadly at the tarnished jewellery box
Which a worm calls home
I swim away from this ship that humans fantasised about.

Steven Houston (10
Carnbroe Primary School

A BIRD'S DREAM

I wake up in my nest
The winter is snowy and frosty
The bitter breeze is whistling through the trees as I fly up
Into the air.

I see the cold fog as I fly
And the people laughing and talking, all wrapped up as I fly
Into the air

I dream of a summer day
And the warmth in my nest
But it will never come and I shall freeze to death
Here in the air

Kirsty Hazlett (10)
Carnbroe Primary School

THE EVACUATION OF ME

My brother faces the open window
But has to turn back when he smells the smoke
He starts to choke and splutter
As I would have done
I ask him to shut the window

I hear the bombs falling
The children crying for their mum and dad
Suddenly I don't feel well
I want to go home.

Finally we got to where we were headed
We get a very nice lady
Who was glad to have us

When I got home my house was no longer there
Neither were my parents.

Rebecca Fingland (10)
Carnbroe Primary School

OUTSIDE US

As soft as feathers
I float all day in the sky
Until the water comes
I drizzle and disappear

The queen of the sky
The sun's young sister
As silver as the finest metal
The brightest thing at night

The fiery giant
Who runs round the earth
And keeps all of the universe
Warm with its flames.

Dale Tyczynski (10)
Carnbroe Primary School

GOING ON HOLIDAY

Early in the morning, getting ready to go.
At the airport,
Seeing the planes,
Big and long.
Men loading all the bags.
My flight is called,
Tickets checked, seats found.
Dreaming of hot sand at the beach.
I drift off to sleep.
Waking up to find,
I hadn't left the ground.

Mari Cullen (11)
Crawforddyke Primary School

MY JOURNEY HOME

As I stepped on to Platform Nine,
Everything looked so fine.
Boys,
Girls,
Men,
Women,
Rushing by.
A little baby starts to cry.
Then comes the noise of the train.
Getting louder,
And louder.
It looks very clean.
It almost seems to gleam.
Big rush to get a good seat.
People falling over their feet.
Ticket Man comes round to check our tickets.
Then off we go on our journey home.
Rattling and rolling over the rails.
Oh how it seems such a lovely day,
Birds, houses, trees, horses passing by.
It's a lovely blue sky.
We're getting closer and
Closer to our destination.
I can see the station just ahead.
The noise of the brakes is very *loud*.
I can't wait to get into my own
Peaceful
House.

Emma Crawford (11)
Crawforddyke Primary School

MY FIRST BOAT JOURNEY

My first boat journey,
Going to Arran,
It was scary,
Frightening,
Very shaky.
I was scared,
I went outside.
I went inside.
It was just the same.
It was a very big ferry boat,
Passengers,
Cars,
Lorries too.
I looked over the side,
Could see the basking sharks,
Far, far out in the sea.
I was scared.
Once we could see Arran,
We all cheered.
When we got off the ferry,
I could still feel myself rocking.
My ferry journey had ended,
But I journeyed on.

Lisa Pithie (11)
Crawforddyke Primary School

MY JOURNEY IN A SUBMARINE

I was sitting in my car,
With my mum and dad.
We were going to pick up my old gran,
And her house was miles away.
I decided to sleep,
Perhaps have a wonderful dream.
What a dream I had!

I was in a submarine,
All by myself
Under the big, blue sea.
Fish passing,
Sharks banging,
Many whales and rocks.
Sharks threatening everyone,
Then I saw a fish going in a hole.
There was a net,
I thought it would get caught
But it came darting onwards.
I was so happy in this place,
But then I woke up.

Beside me was my old gran,
She was just sitting watching me.

Chris J Reilly (11)
Crawforddyke Primary School

ON THE BUS

There's a driver over there,
He's driving very slow.
I wish he would hurry up,
Others are telling him to go!

There's a lady over there,
She's sitting reading her paper.
The bus starts to get busy,
She says, 'I'll see you later.'

There's a baby over there,
She's in her pram.
She's watching everyone
I think she's very calm.

There's a boy over there,
He's sitting in a chair,
Eating a yoghurt,
With a big brown bear.

Emma Taylor (11)
Crawforddyke Primary School

ON THE BEACH

There's a granny over there,
Playing with the sand.
I asked her if she wanted a hand,
But of course, she's listening to a band.

There's a lifeguard over there,
Shouting at the kids.
Because they're being very bad,
And lifting up the bin lids.

There's a policeman over there,
Walking along the beach.
His hat blew off,
So he had to reach.

Stephanie Turnbull (11)
Crawforddyke Primary School

ON THE BEACH

There's a baby over there,
Swimming in the sea,
He'll be alright,
The water goes up to his knee.

There's a crab over there,
It's nipping my mum.
I think she better move,
Her bum's getting numb.

There's a fisherman over there,
Fishing for fish
So he can put one,
In his cat's dish.

There's a man over there,
Eating his lunch.
He better be careful,
Or the birds will give it a munch.

There's a dog over there,
Running through the sea.
He'd better not come,
To dry himself on me.

Steven T Howson (11)
Crawforddyke Primary School

ON THE BUS

There's a boy over there,
Sitting on his seat.
He looks very tired,
Looking at his smelly feet.

There's a girl over there,
Drinking her large can.
She's sitting all alone,
Playing with her fan.

There's a man over there,
He's singing a song.
He's getting off soon,
To go and play Ping-Pong.

There's a driver over there,
He is steering the bus.
He's going very slowly,
But he's getting told to rush.

John Poole (11)
Crawforddyke Primary School

ON THE BEACH

There's a girl over there,
Washing her feet.
With very hot water,
She begins to feel the heat.

There's a baby over there,
Trying to swim.
With his big rubber ring
And everybody is shouting, 'Look at him!'

There's a lady over there,
Washing her hands.
She was sitting next to the rocks,
Covered in sand.

There's my dad over there,
Eating a bun.
On his big beach chair,
Trying to have some fun.

Arlene Jenkins (11)
Crawforddyke Primary School

ON A DESERT ISLAND

There's a monkey over there,
Climbing up a tree.
Trying to get a banana,
For his tea.

There's a snake over there,
Slithering through the sand.
Trying to get a mouse,
It's going for my hand.

There's a spring over there,
I think I'll have a drink.
I'll make a clay cup,
This clay's a little pink!

There are some leaves over there,
I think I'll make a bed.
For when I feel sleepy,
I can lay down my head.

Darren Miller (11)
Crawforddyke Primary School

AT THE STADIUM

There's a linesman over there,
He's holding out his flag.
Everyone boos
And all start to nag.

There's a referee over there,
He pulls out a red card.
The player got told,
He was being too hard.

There's a player over there,
He goes in a huff.
He told the manager,
That he was being too rough.

There's a supporter over there,
He starts to cheer.
I guess it's because
He's had too much beer.

Michelle Burns (11)
Crawforddyke Primary School

ON THE BUS

There's a lassie over there,
She's playing with her hair.
She likes to talk,
To her new friend the bear.

There's a baby over there,
She starts to cry.
I think it is because,
She has poked her eye.

There's a lad over there,
He looks very sad.
I think it is because
He has lost his dad.

There's a dad over there,
He looks very upset.
I think it is because,
He is very wet.

Natasha C Black (11)
Crawforddyke Primary School

IN THE SWIMMING POOL

There's a man over there,
He's washing his hair.
There's a shark swimming around,
He'd better take care.

There's a baby over there,
It's sitting in a high chair.
It's eating an ice lolly,
And pulling its hair.

There's a girl over there,
She's starting to drown.
Nobody's about,
You can see her frown.

There's a lifeguard over there,
He's walking about.
Somebody's bad
And he starts to shout.

Kristy McIlwain (11)
Crawforddyke Primary School

ON THE BEACH

There's a lifeguard over there,
He's looking out to sea.
I wonder if he's going to run in,
After he's had his tea.

There's a lady over there,
I think she's starting to shout.
She better look out,
Because there are bears about.

There's a boy over there,
He's swimming around.
Oh! I think he's starting to drown.
I don't think he can touch the ground.

There's a crab over there,
It's beside my mum.
She better look out,
Because it may nip her bum.

Vyvyan Stratton (11)
Crawforddyke Primary School

ON THE BEACH

There's a lady over there,
She's lying on the sand,
She's screaming in pain,
Because a shark bit off her hand.

There's a boy over there,
He's swimming in the sea,
Although he doesn't know it,
There's an octopus on his knee.

There's a girl over there,
She's running along the beach,
She can feel something cold and slimy,
Because she has stood on a great big peach!

Craig Owens (11)
Crawforddyke Primary School

VOYAGE OF THE PAST

Walking along the docks approaching the boat.
All the slaves loading the crates and bags.
The sailors untying the huge boat to set off on its journey.
The workmen pulling up the sails with a great heave.
The doctor in the medical room healing the injured and sick.
The cook in the kitchen cooking the tea for the strong men.
The captain steering the ship to its final destination.
The sea smacking off the side of the ship with great power.
The wind in the sail pushing the boat along.
The day ending,
Getting darker, darker.
The sky full of twinkling stars and constellations.
Some of the crew go to bed,
While others get up for the night.
The sleepless nights because of all the noise,
Creaking,
Splashing,
Chattering,
Shouts of danger ahead.
The storm approaching, they hope they will survive.

Elliot G Lindsay (11)
Crawforddyke Primary School

In The Stadium

There's a manager over there,
He's training his team
But he said if they win,
It'll be his dream!

There's a player over there,
He would like to play as keeper
And be captain,
But instead he plays as sweeper.

There's a linesman over there,
He is in charge of the offsides.
If there is any he waves his flag,
While he takes big strides.

There's a guard over there,
Keeping the crowd off the pitch.
He tripped over the ball,
And fell down a ditch.

Jamie Brownlee (11)
Crawforddyke Primary School

In The Park

There's a lad over there,
Looking very sad.
His dad is going *mad*,
I think the lad is bad.

There's a mum over there,
Looking very dumb
She is sucking her thumb,
And eating her gum.

There's a man over there,
Looking very hot.
Waving his fan,
And drinking from his can.

There's a boy over there,
He is full of joy.
Sitting on his chair,
Playing with his toy.

Janey Finnie (11)
Crawforddyke Primary School

MY DAD

My dad is very tall
He hates to play football.

He works on the farm
And has a strong arm.

He gives me a hug
And drinks out of a mug.

He cannot cook,
Won't read a book.

He looks after the cows
And rarely bows.
Because he's my wonderful dad!

Margaret Dunbar (10
Gilmourton Primary School

MY FRIEND

One day at school my friend and I were thinking,
We thought it was time that I came up for a day
And we were thinking of all the games we could play.
So when I got home I picked up the phone and dialled my
friend's number.
We arranged to come up on Friday, after school he did say
on that day.
I shouted hooray and started to pack my bags.
At school I waited and waited, for the bell to go.
When it did ring, I wanted to sing but the teacher wouldn't approve.
The children poured out of school we had to walk, that's the rule.
When we got on the bus we made such a fuss because Martin the infant
is late.
When I got to my friend's, we played a lot of games,
On Tomb Raider 3, I shot a baddie and the blood spilled all over the
floor.
It was time for me to go home, but I didn't want to go home,
I didn't want to but my mum said I had to so I said goodbye to
my friend.

Gavin Cowan (10)
Gilmourton Primary School

ANGELS

Flapping angels above the starlit moon
Were getting nearer and nearer,
There will be gladness soon.
We met the emperor at the stable door,
Oh look there's Mary sitting on the floor!
We're happy now the new king's born
Let's go to sleep until it's dawn.

Lauren Johnstone (11)
Gilmourton Primary School

BATTLEFIELD

The battlefield lies silent now,
Dead bodies litter the ground.
Craters the size of buses lie around.
Abandoned tanks smoke away,
The moan of the wounded is the only sound.
The stink of the dead drowns the smell of grass.
Scorched grass around dead men,
Empty cartridges lie behind sandbags.
A faint rifle shot can be heard.
Windowpanes on buildings shattered.
The constant drone of aircraft flying overhead.
The screams of dying men now have passed.
The battlefield lies silent now.

Ross Graham (11)
Gilmourton Primary School

A STREAM IN SPRING

Gently flowing
Dancing water hits my face
Plip, plop the rain is coming
I run home as the stream rises
It floods the fields.
The farmer's sheep rest safely
On a hill.

Days later I'm back down,
The sheep are grazing all around.
I run to the stream, *splash!*
Back to normal I guess.

Janet Anderson (10)
Gilmourton Primary School

THE CHRISTMAS ANGEL

It's sparkling in the snow,
It's floating in the mist.
Its wings are glistening silver.
Its dress is amethyst.
Its golden hair is flowing
        gently in the breeze.
Its halo's shining brightly
        for it is Christmas Eve!

Danielle Campbell (11)
Gilmourton Primary School

MY CAT

My cat is ginger
He goes for your finger.

He sleeps on the chair
But I don't think it's fair.

My cat gets fed four times a day,
Waits for a while then . . . goes out to play.

Morag Russell (9)
Gilmourton Primary School

A GOAL

He kicks the ball high,
It went flying through the air,
The goalie watched it,
The ball was coming back down,
The goalie was not ready.

Craig Ramsay (9)
Gilmourton Primary School

CATS

As my cat sits on the sill, staring out for no real purpose.
I wonder how many cats there are roaming our Earth's surface.

The ginger and white cat lazy and fat
Sleeping soundly on the fireside mat.

The sleek black cat shining in the sunlight
Everyone cries, 'What a wonderful sight!'

The tortoiseshell cat white, brown and black.
For hunting this cat has a special knack.

The snowy white cat as white as snow
Any questions the answers he'll know.

Now you know these cats, their personalities as well
So if someone asks, you'll be able to tell.

Rebecca Hearsey (11)
Gilmourton Primary School

HIM

He is a bossy, boisterous, boring, bad tempered
and very bitter boy.

He talks a lot of bizarre balderdash
which bores other boys to a bewildered bore.

He looks like a beefy, brawny, bedraggled
and very biased baseball bluffer.

And goes berserk if you call him brilliant,
What is he . . .? A brother!

Robyn Gilliland (11)
Gilmourton Primary School

HOLIDAYS

Warm beaches,
Cold pools,
Hot sun,
Nice food,
Smelly taxis,
Theme parks,
Massive waves,
Luxury desserts,
Maybe even
A desert
But best
Of all
School is Off.

Josh Crozer (8)
Gilmourton Primary School

MUM

My mum spoils me so much
When we're in the town,
She buys me clothes, CDs and games
And puts up with the sound.
I love her and she loves me
And that will never change.
Even when she is away I love her
All the same.
But the thing that counts the most of all
Is friendship - that's the best.
We'll stick together side by side,
Because I love her none the less.

Rachel Correlli (11)
Gilmourton Primary School

My Farm

It's a busy life living on a farm,
Spreading the muck in winter to make the grass green.
Spraying the crops with weed spray to get rid of weeds,
Baby lambs and calves needing fed with warm milk,
Summertime comes - it's time to cut the long, juicy, grass
in the fields,
While in the parlour dairy cows are giving milk.
Digging up the potatoes for dinner,
Harvestime comes, the combine comes out
To bring in this year's crop.
Ploughing all the fields for the seed barley
The dogs barking at people going past.

Heather Marshall (11)
Glassford Primary School

Smudge

   I love to feel her
S oft and silky fur.
   watching her
M unching from her bowl. Still
U ntidy and untrained, but that will get better.
   Getting
D irty down on the farm.
G orgeous, with her multi-coloured coat.
E nergetically she looks for her toy mouse.
   Smudge is my best kitten.

Allison Marshall (9)
Glassford Primary School

POP STARS

P erformances are fun to do!
O n the radio people hear my songs.
P retty clothes to wear, it's lovely!

S inging different kinds of songs,
T otally annoyed about not being at number one.
A nxiously I walked on stage.
R ocking and rolling all night long.
S tage performances makes a good warm feeling in my tummy.

Ashleigh Watt (11)
Glassford Primary School

MY DOG RUSTY

R usty-coloured fur that is rough to touch.
U nusual fat, fluffy, long ears.
S illy brown eyes look into mine.
   A little waggy
T ail, hits off the wall.
   Snoring and
Y awning all day long.
   I know he's lazy, but that doesn't stop me loving him.

Rebekah Tait (8)
Glassford Primary School

SPACESHIPS

Sailing through the Milky Way,
Pouring out the rocket gas
Arriving at a super station,
Circling round a red, red planet
Eating strange spaceship food.

Soaring through the open space,
Having fun, but concentrating,
Imagining what's happening on Earth,
Peering through the spaceship window
Sensing all the weird and wonderful things from other planets.

Stephanie Speedie (10)
Glassford Primary School

MY PET CAT

A soft, silky, black and white coat.
Deep, pond-weedy eyes with a round dark centre.
A small, cute face.
A little light pink nose with a tiny mouth.
A long, fluffy, furry tail.
Pointed, alert ears.
Quivering, thin whiskers.
Her name is Mopsy.

Lorna Johnston (9)
Glassford Primary School

CUDDLES

    I love to
C   uddle my soft rabbit. His
U   ntidy face always looks dirty. His long
D   roopy ears reach to the ground.
D   ozy, often falling asleep. He
L   oves to eat vegetables. Big, brown
E   yes, staring back at me.
S   pringing high and low over the green grass.
    I love my rabbit called *Cuddles.*

Gillian Marshall (9)
Glassford Primary School

COLOURS

C rimson leaves,
   hanging from the trees.
O range sun in the sky,
   birds flying very high.
L ilac petals on a flower,
   grows and grows in a very light shower.
O ld black dusty book,
   on the cover, it says *cook.*
U gly grey clouds,
   like huge grey mounds.
R uby red throne in the hall,
   leaning against the bright red wall.
S carlet feathers on the ground,
   when the wind blows, there's a whistling sound.

Sophie Kilby (8)
Glassford Primary School

MY DOG RYATH

   A lovely, dark,
R usty-coloured tail. The
Y oungest dog I've ever had in my life.
   A friendly
A lsatian, all cheery and bright.
   A multi-coloured
T uggy-rope keeps her company at night.
   A short,
H airy coat, like a rough brush.
   Ryath is my kind of dog.

Cassie Morrison (9)
Glassford Primary School

MY DOG PENNY

My dog Penny's a black Labrador, with a jet-black
                                        shining coat.
Huge, brown, saucer eyes that sparkle.
Big, pointy ears that hear every sound,
Her waggy tail is hard and thick, thumping on the ground.
A sad looking face, that hides her happy nature.
Penny has a big appetite,
But is really very skinny
From chasing her toy round and round the fields
                                        which keeps her fit.
After all that she flops down to sleep in front of the radiator.

Emma Crozier (10)
Glassford Primary School

I WISH

I wish I could be a footballer
I wish I could get a hat-trick in every game
I wish I could play in midfield
I wish I could play for the best team
I wish I could meet famous players
I wish I could win the cup
I wish I could be captain
I wish I could celebrate with all my team
I wish I could be the best player in the world
I wish I could make *millions* of pounds
I wish I could be famous!

Ross Clacher 10)
Glassford Primary School

WINTER MORNING

In the cold winter morning
A robin flew down from the shining sky,
To land on freezing, glistening snow
Leaving small frozen footprints behind it.
Fluffy snowflakes falling from the purple sky
Onto the crunchy grass,
And covering the dying plants
With a blanket of white.
No carrots for dinner -
I used them for my sleeping snowman
With its huge body and a tiny head.
No coal for the blazing fire,
The sleeping snowman took it all.
In the icy breeze the hedges shiver
And the cobwebs shimmer with silver
As the garden enjoys its winter sleep.

Ashleigh Fleming (11)
Glassford Primary School

HOLIDAYS

I'd like to go on holiday,
To mess about and have fun,
On the beach is where I'd like to stay,
Chasing waves as I freely run.

I'd like to swim in a deep blue pool,
And sit in a rubber ring,
Eating ice-creams to make me cool,
Relaxing as I sing.

I'd like to go on boat trips,
And look at the beautiful sea,
To sail on big pirate ships,
And watch the fish staring at me.

I'd like to get a golden tan,
Lie and sunbathe every day,
Cooling myself with a fan,
Yes, I'd like a holiday.

Robyn Hasler (11)
Glassford Primary School

WHAT'S RED?

My sore nose as it streams with the cold.
Strong beam of the sun in the summer, making me sweat.
A violent volcano erupting hot lava, exploding from the peak.
The screaming fire engine rushing to the fire.
A beautiful red sky at night making the world bright.
Warm trickle of blood running down my leg from my skinned knee.
Rosy lips that break into a wide smile.
A delicate rosebud in the garden, waiting to be picked.
Warning signs dotted all over the country roads.
Bright tartans to wear on Burns' Night.
A Flanders poppy to remember the war and the people who
                                        lost their lives.
Sweet wine for celebrations.
Holly berries on Christmas wreaths.
Juicy strawberries sitting in a bowl of fresh fruit.
That's red!

Christine Foster (11)
Glassford Primary School

PETS

Pets, pets, I love pets
They're fluffy and cuddly except when they're wet
I'll never forget that I've got pets,
Pets are nice to have.

Pets, pets, I love pets,
I like to play with them,
I feed them and clap them if I can.
If their noses are dry
They are not feeling well
'Mum I want another pet, not to sell.'

Thomas Ritchie (7)
Kirkshaws Primary School

DRAGON

Dragon, dragon, oh mighty dragon
you have beaten them all.

You beat the giant at thumb-wrestling
and the witches at dodge ball.

Dragon, dragon, oh mightiest of them all,
the only thing you'll never do is
beat me at baseball.

Jon Barron (8)
Kirkshaws Primary School

SPACE

In space there are stars,
I would just love to go to Mars,
When the stars are shining bright,
Like little twinkling lights.

When I was in the rocket,
I looked in my pocket,
I found an alien's car,
It was shaped like a star.

When I looked at the comets,
And the planets too,
The stars are shining bright,
Right over you.

Corri O'Reilly (8)
Kirkshaws Primary School

BUTTERFLY

Butterflies, butterflies,
Who likes butterflies?
I do, I do,
I like butterflies.

Butterflies, butterflies,
Who likes butterflies?
In my garden
There are lots of butterflies.

Kate McGibbon (8)
Kirkshaws Primary School

OUR SCHOOL TRIP TO SPACE

I can see stars,
I can see a comet,
Everybody (I think) is going to vomit.

Some people are whizzing,
Some are dizzy,
I've got a sore head
My head feels fizzy.

I've just arrived home,
I'm really tired,
I've been to Mars,
and back.

What's that I can see?
Is that me?
I must be 1003.

Victoria Blades (8)
Kirkshaws Primary School

SPACE

Comets through the night blue sky,
Sparkling aliens oh so high.
Stars are bright, especially at night.
The sun is crackling, the moon is sparkling,
I saw it all with my telescope.

Allan Purves (8)
Kirkshaws Primary School

SCHOOL

School, school
I like school
The teachers are nice
but sometimes cool.
I like the pictures that
we paint in school.
I like to play but I am
very noisy.

The headmaster is good.
He helps us if we fall.
I like school and my
friends best of all.

Lisa Williamson (7)
Kirkshaws Primary School

SPACE

Space, space, space.
Have you been up in space?
I can't go to space
Because I'm in a race.

Space, space, space,
I've been up in space.
I've been to Mars and back again,
Now it will start all over again.

Kirsty McAuley (8)
Kirkshaws Primary School

SCHOOL

School, school,
school, school.

Why do I have to come to school?
We come to school to read and write
But out in the playground
we should not fight.

School, school,
school, school.

Some people are cruel
But not in school.

School, school,
school, school.

I cannot ask for a better school.

Jade Ann McLenachan (8)
Kirkshaws Primary School

SCHOOL

School, school, school
I like school
I love it too
But why do I need to go?
You need to go
To read and write
Then you draw
And paint so bright.

Kelly McGill (8)
Kirkshaws Primary School

FAR OUT AT SEA

Until I saw the sea
I did not know
Lashing winds
    Far out at sea
    White sea foams
On a brave voyage
When the night wind roars
    Far out at sea
    White sea foams
The sun making splinters
In the clear waters
    Far out at sea
    White sea foams
Driving Kingfisher home
Back to France
To celebrate and enjoy.

Stacy McCandless (10)
Newfield Primary School

LONELINESS

Loneliness is when you don't have anyone to play with.
Loneliness is when everyone is inside.
Loneliness is when nobody visits you.
Loneliness is when nobody ever talks to you.
Loneliness is when somebody leaves you by yourself.
Loneliness is when everyone goes away but not you.
Loneliness is when someone dies.

Ashley Potter (9)
Newfield Primary School

THE EAGLE

How he spends his day
Soaring high over the
Highlands,
His big brown eyes
Watching his prey
As he swoops down
To kill
A poor earth-born companion
With his dagger claws!
He is proud,
A bold,
A wonderful bird
As he drifts off into
The sunset to go back to
His nest to feed.

Rachel Miller (11)
Newfield Primary School

TIGERS

T   igers like to pounce on their prey and don't let other tigers
    get to play.
I   don't think the tiger will be sleeping today.
G   obbling up his dinner, a zebra, is very nice.
E   ye to eye to another tiger, ready to pounce, fighting for food.
R   acing through the woods trying to pounce on its prey.
S   leeping, very tired, all day long, it fights for its prey.

Lisa Dyer (11)
Newfield Primary School

THE PINK PIG

T he pink pig strolling about looking for mud,
H e rolls all day in the dirty brown mud,
E ven when it's dinner time, he looks for mud!

P ig is fat with his squashy nose looking for food,
I n the house there may be mud,
N o! Pig does not like staying clean
K ind and gentle he may be!

P ig is pig and that's what he wants to be.
I n the farm that's all he does, rolls about in the mud.
'G o away,' the pigs may say, so pink pig walks away.
   That's pig!

Kelly Hamilton (11)
Newfield Primary School

THUMPER MY RABBIT

Thumper is my rabbit,
Me and my sisters share him,
We all love him so much,
We hope he doesn't go soon.
He is a big rabbit with long floppy ears,
He is light brown and white
With a little bit of grey.
Thumper is an old rabbit,
He is about seven years old,
He likes to run around the garden
And doesn't like it when it's time to go home!

Kim Graham (11)
Newfield Primary School

FAR OUT AT SEA

Far out at sea
white sea foam.
The sun making splinters
in a whole sea of blue.
Until I saw the sea
I did not know.
Lashing winds
far out at sea.
White sea foam.
The sea like a hungry monster,
hush-hushing,
chill-rushing.
On an amazing voyage,
driving Kingfisher back home to France
to celebrations of joy.

Amanda Millar (10)
Newfield Primary School

HUNTING TIGER

When a tiger needs his dinner,
He sneaks with force and terror,
To kill his powerless prey,
That's not so far away.
He creeps behind a tree,
So it could clearly see,
Where his food would be.
And suddenly he jumps up
To slay his prey like a broken cup.
He gobbles it in a rapid way
So no one shares his tasty prey.

Mohamady El-Gaby (11)
Newfield Primary School

THE AMAZING VOYAGE

Far out at sea
White sea foam
The sun making splinters
In a whole sea of blue
Until I saw the sea
I did not know
Lashing winds
On an amazing voyage.
When the night wind roars
And the moon rocks the clouds
Driving Kingfisher back to France
To celebrations of joy.

Christopher Kane (10)
Newfield Primary School

THE KINGFISHER

The sea,
Like a hungry monster,
Waiting to pounce,
A tiger roaring,
A snarling ocean of
White sea foam
Ready to attack
The Kingfisher
The sea driving the Kingfisher
Home
Back to France.

Hyder Fattah (11)
Newfield Primary School

FAR OUT AT SEA

White sea foam
The sun making splinters
In a whole sea of blue.

Until I saw the sea
I did not know
The long-rolling,
Slow-sliding,
Chill-rushing,
Hush-hushing,
Deep and dangerous waters.
Far out at sea
On the way back to France.

Mark Dunn (11)
Newfield Primary School

FAR OUT AT SEA

Far out at sea
White sea foam
The sun making
Splinters in a whole sea of blue.
The sea like a hungry monster
Waiting to pounce
Far out at sea
Until I saw the sea
I did not know
Crashing winds blow
Back home in France.

Jonathan Morrison (11)
Newfield Primary School

THE AMAZING VOYAGE

Far out at sea
The white sea foams the seam like a HM
The sun splinters a whole sea of blue
Until I saw the sea
I did not know
Lashing winds
On an amazing voyage
When the night roars
And the moon rocks the clouds
Driving Kingfisher home
Back to France.

James McGill (11)
Newfield Primary School

TRAPPED IN MY SHOE

Here in Base 8
One afternoon I got my finger stuck in my shoe
I was pull-pulling, push-pushing,
Hop-hopping, slide-sliding.
On an amazing journey to the school office
Until I saw Mrs Murphy
Who eased my finger out of my shoe!
My finger was scarlet-red for about five minutes
Throb-throbbing.

Steven Forrest (10)
Newfield Primary School

EVERY DAY IS A HAPPY DAY

Every day is a happy day.
Waiting for the bus with Fern.
Going to the brook,
Bathing in the moist mud.
Going for a walk with Fern,
Sleeping in her doll's pram.
Getting milk from a bottle.
Sitting on the bottom step of the stairs
Waiting for Fern.
Fern putting him to bed,
Sleeping in a box of straw.
Under the apple tree
At apple blossom time.

Lisa Thomson (9)
Newfield Primary School

FAR OUT AT SEA

I didn't know lashing winds
Lashed and seas flowed
On an amazing journey
Out at sea where the wind howled.

Sea whispered and rushing waves
Until I saw the sea I did not know
The long-rolling, slow-sliding,
Chill-rushing, hush-hushing and
Deep, dangerous sea thrashed waters.
Far out at sea.

Darren Sommerville (11)
Newfield Primary School

SPACE TRAVEL

S pace suit really heavy
P eople came and watched the rocket go off
A man said to me 'Don't be scared'
C ost my mum and dad £100
E arth had to get left behind

T ight little rooms in the rocket
R eady to stop at the moon
A rrived eventually, ready to go
V enus was the best view
E arth was far away
L eaving now, oh no!

Melanie McKinlay (8)
Newfield Primary School

SPRINGTIME

S pring is here, hip hip hooray.
P etals on flowers all different colours.
R ich rosy apples on the green trees.
I n the air, love is floating.
N eat little shoots showing from earth.
G etting ready to play with some friends.
T ime to go to bed, we go *boo!*
I n the morning we wake up.
M um puts out the washing.
E very afternoon we play out. Yippee!

Lisa Sommerville (8)
Newfield Primary School

THE SEA

The sea is like a hungry monster.
The long, rolling, unbroken waves
Far out at sea.
Slow-sliding
White sea foam.
The sun making splinters of water
Hush-hushing,
Far out at sea.
Deep, dangerous,
The Kingfisher
Sailed.

Sarah-Jane Hunter (10)
Newfield Primary School

FAR OUT AT SEA

Far out at sea
The wind lashing round me.
Pushing the boat further out to sea
Brave Helen still sailing.
The waves blowing very strong
Then I sailed through it
And I celebrated the victory.

Stephen Stewart (10)
Newfield Primary School

THE VOYAGE

Far out at sea
White sea foam,
The sun making splinters
In a whole sea of blue.
The Kingfisher is on a journey
And is testing endurance,
The waves driving Kingfisher home,
To celebrations of joy.
Far out at sea
White sea foam.

Sean Gilfillan (10)
Newfield Primary School

FAR OUT AT SEA

The sun is like a hungry monster,
the long, rolling, unbroken waves
far out at sea,
slow-sliding,
chill-rushing,
hush-hushing,
far out at sea
the Kingfisher
sailed.

Laura Millar (10)
Newfield Primary School

THE PHOENIX AT NIGHT

O phoenix, how you fly so high,
Spreading your magic through the night-time sky.
Your gold and red feathers glitter in the moon,
As you swoop down at the stroke of noon.
Now it's time to rest your wings as you burn out,
Tonight you shall rise again up in the air to fly again.

Ross Jack (11)
Newfield Primary School

ON A SUMMER DAY

The beach was very warm
And I went in the water for a swim.
I went up on the sand to sunbathe.
When I had had a sunbathe
I went to swim in the water again,
Then my mam called me up to go home.

Nicky McCaskie (8)
Newfield Primary School

AUTUMN

A t autumn the leaves start to fall.
U p the trees the squirrels start to sleep.
T he wind blows harder.
U nder the leaves hedgehogs curl up.
M ostly rains, but I don't mind.
N obody likes autumn but I don't mind it at all.

Craig Stenhouse (9)
Newfield Primary School

SUMMER

S   unny, sunny days
U   nder palm trees it is shady
M   ermaids swim about in the sea
M   ad people running about the beach
E   veryone has a chocolate ice cream
R   ides are mad and the rollercoaster is crazy.

Happy days!

Shona Johnston (8)
Newfield Primary School

SUMMER

S   un is bright, it's a very good sight.
U   mbrellas unseen till rain comes near.
M   other's cheering, hooray, hooray, hooray!
M   um's baking lovely cakes.
E   verything beautiful and bright.
R   eally boring, summer is over.

Ailsa Anderson (8)
Newfield Primary School

SUMMER

S   un all day in the sky
U   mbrella not needed, put it away
M   um making muffins all day long
M   uck on the floor from the kids
E   xcited all the day
R   unning in and out of the pool.

Aiden Rogers (8)
Newfield Primary School

LONELINESS

Loneliness is when you don't have any friends
Loneliness is when your mum and dad go on holiday without you
Loneliness is when nobody visits you
Loneliness is when people leave you out
Loneliness is when nobody believes you
Loneliness is when somebody you love dies
Loneliness is when you fall out with friends
Loneliness is when you are in hospital with nobody you know
Loneliness is when you are locked outside
Loneliness is when you are lost in the dark
Loneliness is when you move to a new house
Loneliness is no fun.

David Hamilton (9)
Newfield Primary School

SOUNDS AND SMELLS OF SUMMER

Lilacs bloom on the grass
Birds tweet high up in the wonderful sky
Bees zoom right past your face as they buzz
Sweet sounds of the birds twittering
Butterflies flap in the air
Soft grass on the ground
Sun shining in your face
Paddling pools, splashing with fun
Flowers smell of sweet honey
These are the sounds and smells of summer.

Tom Melvin (9)
Newfield Primary School

SOUNDS AND SMELLS OF SUMMER

Birds in the sky singing all day long
Bees buzzing as they go zooming past
Barbecues sizzling and smells of smoky bacon
Flowers tall and nice to see
Grass growing longer and longer
Butterflies, colourful and beautiful
Ladybirds growing lots of spots
Sun shining all day
Water in rivers going past
Paddling pools - jump in and splash
Apple blossom on the trees
These are the sounds and smells of summer.

Laura Kirkland (9)
Newfield Primary School

SMELLS OF THE FARM

The smells of the farm
The perspiration of tired horses
The smell of axle grease
The smell of rubber boots
The smell of a new rope
The smell of hay
The smell of manure
The smell of slops
The smell of grain and harness
The wonderful sweet breath of patient cows.

Caroline Wilson (9)
Newfield Primary School

THE SOUNDS AND SMELLS OF SWEET SUMMER

The sweet smells of lilacs blooming
Apple blossom on the trees
Flowers that smell sweetly
The sound of bees buzzing by
Butterflies fluttering and flapping their wings
The sound of grass growing
Birds singing soft and sweet
The smoky smell of barbecues
The sound of water dripping
The sound of laughter in paddling pools
The sun shining beneath the trees
These are the sounds and smells of summer.

Asten Hill (9)
Newfield Primary School

PILLS

There was a man who swallowed a pill
and ended up very ill.
He was 107
and went to heaven.
After eleven years in heaven,
he finally went to prison.
 After that he swallowed a cat
and then yelled 'Drat!'

Andrew Payne (8)
Newfield Primary School

SOUNDS AND SMELLS OF SUMMER

Lilacs blooming in the sun
Apple blossom smells sweet and fun
Bees buzzing
Birds singing in the sky
Flowers are getting high
Butterflies fly quite fast
Grass growing and getting long
Barbecues with sizzling steak
Paddling pools are everywhere
Water splashing in the air
Sun shining up above
These are the sounds and sweet smells of summer.

Jenna Browning (9)
Newfield Primary School

SOUNDS AND SMELLS OF SUMMER

Bees buzzing in the air
Birds flying high in the sky
Apple blossom on the colourful trees
Butterflies fluttering over there
Fresh grass all around
Sausages sizzling on the hot barbecue
Children splashing in the cool water
These are the sounds and smells of summer.

Andrew Leckenby (9)
Newfield Primary School

Summer Is Here

S   ummer is here. Cheer, cheer, cheer!
U   mbrellas away in a box, not to be seen till summer stops.
M   um sunbathing in the sun and your sister doing the same.
M   ostly not raining, the sun's taken its place.
E   arly in the morning the sun rises once again to say good morning
    to everyone.
R   ich, shining apples hanging on the trees.

Ashleigh Brown (8)
Newfield Primary School

Loneliness

Loneliness is when I have no one to play with
Loneliness is when nobody talks to me
Loneliness is when my friends go away
Loneliness is when I am lost
Loneliness is when I get bullied and nobody helps me
Loneliness is when nobody believes me.

Alix Reid (9)
Newfield Primary School

My Dog Babe! (Rap)

My dog's name's Babe
She doesn't live in a cage
She sleeps on a bed upstairs.

My mum says it's her baby
So don't be a scared - sadie
It's going to be here all your days.

Gillian Haddow (11)
Newfield Primary School

MARK THE DOG

Black, brown,
Mark the dog.
Stupid and ugly,
Mark the dog.

Acts very smart,
Mark the dog.
Isn't really,
Mark the dog.

Fleas and nits itch his back,
Mark the dog.
Scratches them off,
Mark the dog.

Loves candyfloss,
Mark the dog.
Hates Pedigree Chum,
Mark the dog.

Dumb he might be,
Mark the dog.
He's the coolest,
Mark the dog!

Andrew Murray (11)
Newfield Primary School

MY FATHER

My father is cool,
My father is cruel.
He likes a cheer,
And a beer
At new year.
My father is funny,
And a honey.
He goes to work
To get a wage.
After school
He has a rage.
He has a white car,
And likes driving it far.
He likes his sleep,
And at dinner
Likes not a peep.

Aimee Raeside (9)
Noble Primary School

ICE CREAM

Ice cream is nice
And doesn't taste like rice.
It is really cool
In a swimming pool.
I start to scream
When I see ice cream.
Oh yes it's supreme
When I get ice cream.
It really tastes nice with a flake
And a big chocolate milk shake.

Ashleigh Aitchison (9)
Noble Primary School

SANTA

Santa is on the way
With his heavy sleigh,
Coming to bring girls and boys
Some lovely playful Christmas toys.

All year through
He is watching you,
Trying to see
Who nice will be.
Are you playing in your room?
Are you playing in your school?

Have you been good?
Have you been bad?
Have you been happy?
Have you been sad?

Santa's here.

Hannah Callander (8)
Noble Primary School

SANTA

Ho . . . Ho . . . Ho,
Santa's on his way!
He's coming through the snow in his sleigh,
He's coming to bring some toys
For some girls and boys.
Christmas Day
Is when Santa's away.
Let us all pray
For him to stay
For next year!

Emma Blue (8)
Noble Primary School

MERRY CHRISTMAS

C is for Christmas.
H is for holly.
R is for Rudolph.
I is for ice.
S is for Santa.
T is for tree.
M is for mistletoe.
A is for apples.
S is for snow.

Shanon Cook (8)
Noble Primary School

MY FATHER

My father is cool
And he walks me to school.
He likes to jump in a pool,
But sometimes he's cruel.
He likes to have a drink
And he hates the colour pink.

Danielle Mullen (9)
Noble Primary School

CHEER

Christmas time is full of cheer,
A time when all our friends are near.
Christmas time is a giving time,
A sharing, loving, caring time
As we remember the birth of a king,
Around the Christmas tree we sing.

Vivian Miller (8)
Noble Primary School

MA FITBA TEAM

Ma fitba teams playin' the day,
The same as we play every Saturday.
The other team are rarin' tae go
But we're gonna beat them but they don't know.

I came in with a header
And passed it tae ma mate,
He kicked it a blooter
Right into the net.

We won 1-0 at the end of the day,
I cannae wait tae next week when we come back tae play.

Andrew Lennox (9)
Noble Primary School

FOOTBALL

I always play football with my friends at school.
We play football because it's cool.
I play with a football team, we are very good,
But when we lose at football we get in a bad mood.
Our manager began to call,
But we'd lost the ball.
One day I scored an overhead kick,
Everyone said it was a real neat trick.
Last year our team was top of the league,
But after the games we suffered from fatigue.

Jordan Ferguson (9)
Noble Primary School

MY BEST FRIEND

I have a friend called Heather
And she really makes me laugh.
She is always there beside me,
People call her my other half.

Heather's hair is golden
But my hair is brown.
When we have a falling out
It always makes her frown.

Every time I see her
She has a great big smile,
Compared to any other friend
She'll beat them by a mile.

Heather McAlpine (9)
Noble Primary School

CHRISTMAS

I love Christmas.
I love snow.
I love December.
I love Santa, Rudolph and the elves.
I love all the presents I get.

I help my dad
To put up the tree,
To put up the baubles
And a special fairy.

Jordan Meharry (8)
Noble Primary School

MY MUM

My mum can be fun
But only when everything's done.
When I eat lots of goods
She goes in all kinds of moods.
When I asked for extra money
She always thinks I'm being funny.
Sometimes she eats late at night
And then comes up and gives me a fright.
When I say I'm going out
She runs about, screams and shouts.
My mum really is the best
So I think she should put her feet up
                              and have a rest.

Kirsty Lawrie (9)
Noble Primary School

CHRISTMAS

C is for the birth of Christ.
H is for how special that it is.
R is for a really merry Christmas.
I   is for the icing on the Christmas cake.
S is for the stable that Jesus was born in.
T is for trying to go back to sleep on Christmas Eve.
M is for the most special Christmas.
A is for all the people being happy at Christmas.
S is for a really silent Christmas.

Kirstin Tait (8)
Noble Primary School

FRIENDS

F riends are cool,
R espect each other.
I love friends.
E very friend is cool.
N ever fall out.
D on't go away with somebody.
S ensational friends.

Kris McArthur (9)
Noble Primary School

SPACE

Last month I went to a race,
It obviously happened in space.
I sped up the pace,
Then I fell onto my face,
I had forgotten to tie my lace.
When the race was over
I found a four-leaved clover.

Gary Wilson (9)
Noble Primary School

CONES

Cones are cool,
Especially in a pool,
Even with a flake,
Then I start to shake.
I eat them in the sun,
But I think cones
Are
Cool.

Jamie N Kelly (9)
Noble Primary School

BELLS AT CHRISTMAS

On a Christmas sleigh
We give ourselves to play.
We can always sing
To the bells that ring.
Jingle bells,
Santa's bells,
Christmas bells,
Church bells,
We can watch as we sway
Because this is Christmas Day.

Susan McRae (8)
Noble Primary School

A VIKING VOYAGE

Vikings went to Scotland,
At dawn they came.
The Vikings got into their long ships
And set off.
They looked like very fierce warriors
With long beards.
They landed on the surface,
All the people were scared,
They didn't know what to do,
They were dressed in dirty, smelly rags.
The Vikings stared to raid the land.
The Vikings and the people came face to face.

Lauren Lynn (10)
Old Monkland Primary School

A VIKING VOYAGE

They are preparing for a feast will soon be here.
Vikings go a-raiding, mud all in their hair.
Ready to set off at dawn,
Soon they will be gone.

Blood-thirsty boys killing for loot,
Stabbing daggers in their heart,
No one even dares to part.

Vikings stealing slaves to trade,
They don't want to be paid.
The feast is taking part,
Loving families with not much heart.

Jenna Swan (10)
Old Monkland Primary School

A VIKING VOYAGE

I can see the Vikings coming,
They are scary and fierce,
They are coming to battle Scotland.

They are coming closer and closer to me,
I'm scared, they have sharp swords to cut us,
They have killed my friend, Annie.
Now they are going away,
They are in the boat heading home.

Stephanie Woods (10)
Old Monkland Primary School

A VIKING VOYAGE

I was just going to bed that night,
I went to the window to check outside.
There was something with oars,
And shields on the side.

The boat was so big, with a huge red sail,
Looked like a dragon with a great big tail.

They came ashore, ran across the bay,
I was so scared I had nothing to say.
They captured the monks, took all their gold,
They took us as slaves, we'll surely be sold.

Amy Calderwood (10)
Old Monkland Primary School

A VIKING VOYAGE

They had a red sail
Put up with a nail.
The brown oars
Had brown pores.

Stabbing daggers in their heart,
No one ever dared to part.
The feast still took part
Even though they hadn't got a heart.

Ashley Stewart (9)
Old Monkland Primary School

A Viking Voyage

Vikings were bad,
They'd make you sad,
And you'd make them mad
And they'd take you away
And make you their slave.

Vikings stole gold and silver
But they needed slaves
So when they went on a raid
They also took slaves.

After a raid if it was good
They would have a feast,
The slaves would have made the food.

Ross Richardson (10)
Old Monkland Primary School

A Viking Voyage

In Norway as they say goodbye,
Their children and families hope they don't die.

During the raid they steal some men,
They killed some and one was called Ben.

A man was so stupid on the way back,
He squeezed a dead body into his brown sack.

Adam Skinner (9)
Old Monkland Primary School

A VIKING VOYAGE

The Vikings had a boat that had a prow
And the little boy told how
To make the boat scary,
No it is not supposed to be like a fairy.
The Scots are against the Vikings,
Scots died, Vikings lived.
The Vikings took gold, silver, food
And treasure and then they went back.
They left Scots to die outside their homes
And the women went to Norway to be slaves
And that's what happened.

Scott Ward (9)
Old Monkland Primary School

A VIKING VOYAGE

I can see Vikings big and fierce,
They always keep on going off
In search of slaves for their boats.
They always keep on coming and going,
They always go to Norway, Sweden,
Finland and Denmark.
They sailed their boats
And took them out on the sea,
You wouldn't be glad if they got you.

Nicola Brady (10)
Old Monkland Primary School

PARENTS' LOVE

It happens in Scotland, England and Wales,
It happens in Ireland too.
It happens in countries all over the world,
But there's little the kids can do.

They go to bed with crying eyes,
And tears streaming down their face.
They sometimes dream of happy days,
But they wake up in a horrible place.

A broken leg, a fractured arm,
After falling down the stairs?
Returning from school to an empty house,
Their parents are never there.

Heather Baillie (11)
Plains Primary School

OLD MAN

On the streets day and night,
Living in a box, raking bins for food.
Finding useless bits of paper,
Sometimes lucky enough to find food.
When you're like me, anything is good.
Sitting on a corner next to a pub,

People give me loose change,
All I want is a can of lager.

Jamie Martin (11)
Plains Primary School

ON THE STREETS

A sit at the side o' Woolworth's,
A don't no whit tae dae,
A fun a stane in ma shoe,
It's jammed between ma tae.

A jist hid taen ma soak aff,
An laid it oan the grun,
Alang came a wee broone dug,
An taen ma soak fur fun!

A stood up in ma bare feet,
Ma face wis rid wi rage,
Fur whit that dug did tae me,
It should be locked up in a cage!

People hiv stood an watched me
But naebody really cares,
So a went back and sat at Woolworth's
An jist laid doon an' said ma prayers.

Cheryl MacDonald (11)
Plains Primary School

HOMELESS

H ow did I end up homeless,
O ot in the street aw night?
M aybe I should a listened to ma ma' and da'.
E xcept no' me! (Am always right),
L iving in an auld warehoose,
E ating oot o' people's bins.
S oon I hope tae go home.
S orry Ma', forgive ma sins.

Chris Arbuckle (11)
Plains Primary School

A Dug's Life

It's sometimes guid tae be a dug
I get fed three times a day.
Running through fields,
With other dogs tae play.

I have a kitchen as a hame.
Every time I want food, it is always the same.
Pedigree Chum and Breath Busters,
Tit bits from people's plates.

I want the cat next door tae bite it,
An' rip it tae little bits.
Then it will run away scared.
An' never come out when I'm there.

It's sometimes guid tae be a dug,
Loads o' cuddles and plenty of love.
Wrapped in ma own wee blanket.
Snug as a bug in a rug!

Jamie Meechan (10)
Plains Primary School

Unhappy Bairn

Every morn' when I get out ma bed
I think aboot the day ahead.
A slap on the lug, a kick on the leg,
That's the best I ever get!
I've got bruises, I've got cuts,
But I've still no' got the guts tae tell.

Andrew Gibb (11)
Plains Primary School

BATTERED BAIRNS

It happens in Scotland
And other places too.
How badly we treat oor weans.
How wid you feel if it was you?

Being battered and bruised.
Used like a punch bag each day.
They're oot a' day an' night.
Some dugs are treated better than they.

Their mithers an faithers don't care aboot them.
Slapping them onay way they can.
Some abuse them so much.
Ye widnae think they were kin.

Kids in this age shouldn'ae be gittin hut.
Sometimes they hit them until they're bruised an' bleeding.
They cry an cry a' night.
When they're left begging an' pleading.

How wid you feel if it was you
Being hut by your faither a' the time?
For weans that are being battered an' abused
It really is a crime

Gael White (10)
Plains Primary School

APPALLED!

It's appalling what is happening,
To children everywhere.
Some live in bins and rubbish tips,
And folk don't even care!

Scott Mitchell (11)
Plains Primary School

TRUE OR FALSE?

True or false?
I saw the green men.
True or false?
They came to me at night.
True or false?
They tried to take our planet.
True or false?
They went for us as well.
True or false?
They transported themselves to their own planet.
True or false?
They never came back again,
Or did they?

Stuart MacFarlane (11)
Plains Primary School

A DUG'S LIFE

It's a delight tae be a dug,
Wi' wee bairns aboot the hoose.
Ma coat gets brushed every day,
An' I get ma dinner made for me.
The only thing I hate a bath,
But if I'm good I get a treat!
I get cosy on Ma's lap, by the fire,
I fall asleep nae bother,
But Ma wakes me up at the drop of a hat,
When she gets up to make a cup of tea!

Stephenie Condron (11)
Plains Primary School

MY MESSY BEDROOM

My bedroom is as messy as a pigsty,
When you open the door you'll find clothes on the floor.
There are more under the bed, some are red.
My teddies are happy, none are snappy.
My rug on the floor is blue and red, it is near the bed.

Harry Hamilton (9)
Robert Smillie Memorial Primary School

PROBLEMS OF MY ROOM

As I slide open my sliding wardrobes they squeak.
My teddies are as cute as a cuddly cat.
My television is as black as a bat,
My bed covers are as purple as a pansy
And my hi-fi is as silver as silver, slippery, shiny treasure.

Emma Thomson (10)
Robert Smillie Memorial Primary School

MY BEDROOM

My bed is red like the hat on my head.
When you open my door you will find clothes on the floor.
My TV is cool don't be a fool
And in my bedroom I rule.

Mark Douglas (10)
Robert Smillie Memorial Primary School

MY AMAZING BEDROOM

My canopy is as beautiful as a dancing dolphin.
My shelves are as long as a giraffe's neck.
My teddies are as furry as a big, brown bear.
My CD player is as noisy as a hyena's laugh
And under my bed my treasure lies.
A necklace with pearls and diamonds like the sparkling
                              stars in the sky.

Stephanie Hammel (10)
Robert Smillie Memorial Primary School

MY BEDROOM

When you open the door
You'll see clothes on the floor.
My room has a creaky floor,
In my room everyone rules no more
And on my bed I have my treasure
My Pikachu teddy.

Lisa Hamilton (10)
Robert Smillie Memorial Primary School

MY BEDROOM

When you open my wardrobe door
All my clothes fall on the floor.
My old TV is fizzy
My big double bed is as bouncy
As a big blown up balloon.

In my drawers my clothes
Are as muddy as dogs' paws.
Tick-tock goes my clock
Time for school again!

Gemma Craw (10)
Robert Smillie Memorial Primary School

MY BEDROOM

My bed is big, black and has covers as blue as the sea
And on my bed sits a teddy that sleeps with me.
On my window hangs curtains as pink as a pig
And next to my bed stands drawers as black as night.
I have a wardrobe as white as snow that stands on a carpet
                                         as green as grass.
In a corner there is a cupboard as thin as a slice of paper
And in it I can only fit a toy box with all my toys in it.

Rachelle Waugh (10)
Robert Smillie Memorial Primary School

MY BEDROOM

My bedroom is as tidy as Heaven,
I have football funny wallpaper.
My door is covered in stickers,
There is one window washed.
My carpet is blue and red too.
I feel cool in my room.
It's the best place I've been
It's true, it's true.

Russell Pate (10)
Robert Smillie Memorial Primary School

MY BEDROOM

My bed is pink and white,
That is where I sleep at night.
My teddy is as white as snow,
The love hearts are as red as Po.
Sitting is my baby doll,
She sits and leans against the wall.
The wardrobe squeaks and creaks
And eeks like a mouse in pain.
The noises drive me insane.
The small toys surround my bed,
The pillow is where I lay my head.

Kayleigh Hamilton (10)
Robert Smillie Memorial Primary School

MY BEDROOM

My bed is big and bouncy
Like a bouncy castle.
My wardrobe is as white as a cloud.
My clock is as white as a cat
And is round like a ball.
My video is very like a vase.
My wrestling ring is flat like a pancake.
My calendar is cool with lots of colours.
My CD player is noisy as an explosion.
My carpet is as colourful as my clock.

William McIlvaney (10)
Robert Smillie Memorial Primary School

MY BEDROOM

My bed is big and bouncy like a bouncy castle.
My wardrobe is white and as wide as an elephant.
My calendar is cool and comes from Cardiff.
My wrestlers are tiny like a mouse.
My PlayStation is as grey as my papa's hair.
My CD player is as noisy as a bomb exploding.
My wrestling ring is as flat as a piece of paper.
My carpet is clean and very colourful.

Gary Houston (10)
Robert Smillie Memorial Primary School

THE TIME MACHINE

T he time machine has been made
H ear the gold bells ringing in the square
E verybody jump for Old Father Time

T he gang of three has now found out
I n some time, they will shout
M aggie is on holiday, what will she say?
E ver been back in time or even to the future?

M any people will say
A neela, Billie, Maggie hoorah!
C ome and see what others have not
H ere in the wondrous year 9999.
I n the year where green flowers grow
N ew-born years are about to unfold
E very time we can hold pictures of the future!

Louise McCulloch (10)
St Aidan's Primary School

I WANT A DOG

I've moaned and groaned because I really want one,
My auntie says you have one, but it's not the same when
It doesn't stay in my very own house.

I've asked and asked, really a lot
I want one, I want one, I do
Please can I have one, I'll look after it too.
I'll buy it a lead and food, it can even stay in my room.
Please can I have one?
Please, please, please, please.

Mum and Dad, I hope you like this poem
Because I really want a dog of my very own.

Jennifer Lynch (10)
St Aidan's Primary School

TRANSPORT

T rains and trams were invented by people,
R iver boats go on rivers.
A ir ships float in the air and if you look down you will see the cities.
N arrow boats, people live on them on the river,
S hips take people overseas for their holidays.
P eople use a lot of transport to get around.
O range trains go fast over the countryside.
R ain thumps down on the vehicles as they travel.
T rucks carry goods from place to place
and people use them a lot.

Jack Friskey (8)
St Aidan's Primary School

MY HOT AIR BALLOON

I was high up in the sky
In my colourful hot air balloon.
It's pink and blue and orange,
Violet, green and yellow.

Over Wales, Paris and Greece,
In my slow large hot air balloon.
I've been flying round for ages,
One year, five weeks, nine minutes.

Now I'm coming straight back home,
From my journey in my hot air balloon
Back to Scotland where I live,
In my colourful, slow, large hot air balloon.

Marta Zadruzynska (9)
St Aidan's Primary School

SPRINGTIME

Springtime is here
Starting off a new year,
Birds on the trees
Hear the buzzing of the bees.
Daffodils, crocus and bluebells are blooming
Long, hot summer days are looming.
Baby chicks are clucking
Leaves now returning
Blue cloudless skies
Winter finally dies.

Louise McLean (11)
St Aidan's Primary School

AN OLD GYPSY CARAVAN

An old tiny gypsy caravan
Travelling from place to place
Looking out at the countryside
At a very slow pace.

We don't stay anywhere
We are always on the move
We love to explore everywhere
Our journey is very smooth.

We have great big horses
We only stay at campsites for a day or two.
Our horses always keep us moving
When we go past we hear the cows moo.

Riding through the town
Riding through the country
Riding round everywhere
Riding round the world.

Andrew Ashe (9)
St Aidan's Primary School

WHAT ARE THE CLOUDS?

The clouds are snowballs rolling down a hill.
They are fluffy pillows on a bed.
They are potatoes in a basin.
They are sheep's wool in a farmer's farm.
They are some ghosts floating in the sky.
They are white fur in my house.

James Bradley (8)
St Aidan's Primary School

THE TIME MACHINE

T he time machine goes swoosh and woop
H e changes shape like a big ball of goop.
E very day he changes colour, red, green, blue.

T he time machine has a siren
I t sounds like a rolling hoop.
M y time machine has lots of buttons
E ven one to change the time.

M y time machine is really cool
A n adventure every day.
C ome with me!
H ave a blast!
I n the past!
N ow come on and have some fun.
E veryone loves it.

Melissa Clare (10)
St Aidan's Primary School

WHAT ARE THE CLOUDS

The clouds are big white pillows
On a blue bed.

They are lots of snow
On some ice.

They are polar bears
In a blue igloo.

Alison Fulton (8)
St Aidan's Primary School

MY TWO GUINEA PIGS

I have two guinea pigs
Which are 5 months old
One called Spike
The other Roddy.

Roddy's always cheeky
Spike hides under the hay
One thing in common
They're both big rascals.

They're always biting our jumpers
So we have to tap their noses
Both of them are cute
And good as could be.

I've told you about Spike
I've told you about Roddy,
Nobody likes guinea pigs
As much as me.

Ciara Donnelly (10)
St Aidan's Primary School

A GREAT CARAVAN

I have a colourful caravan
In the middle of the countryside
And every time we've got to move
I run to get a ride.

We could explore the world in our Caravan
Canada, China or Germany
And when I go to send a postcard
It's from far, far away.

I like my little caravan
It's small and well decorated
And when we went to Arran in it
I made a friend right there.

David Welsh (9)
St Aidan's Primary School

MY DOG

My dog is called Prince
He's only a puppy
He chews on a bone
He is lovely and furry.

If you give him a treat
He'll go straight to his basket
He loves lots of company
When he sleeps all alone.

I'll love him forever
And ever and ever.
He was bought as a surprise
I felt I'd won a prize.

Now he is bigger
He's stronger than me
I wish he was still a puppy
Not up to my knees.

The summer is coming
We'll have lots of fun.
Together we'll play
Then relax in the sun.

Jonathan Dalziel (10)
St Aidan's Primary School

MY TWO LITTLE SISTERS

My two little sisters
Are younger than me
One called Gina
The other Jodie.

Jodie's always happy
Gina's always fun
One thing in common
We all love our mum.

Jodie's just a baby
And Gina's eight years old.
Both are really funny
And both as good as gold.

Now I've told you about Gina
I've told you about Jodie
That was my poem
It sounded more like a story.

Carla Leith (10)
St Aidan's Primary School

MY GREEN BICYCLE

As fast as fast goes my green bike
Nothing can beat it not even my trike
My green bike is very fast
In a race it would never come last.

There's nothing like my bike you see
No one's got it apart from me.
It goes speeding down the hill
And once I bumped right into Uncle Bill.

My bike's great!
It's much better than a roller skate.
Sometimes on it I just sit
Oh I'll be sad when I grow out of it.

Monica Donnelly (9)
St Aidan's Primary School

MY CAT

My cat its name is Tiger
She's a tortoiseshell
And she is very young.
My cat has a lot of meals
Some days she has large fish
That's okay, because she has a big dish.

When my cat wants *in*
She will let you know,
She will sit on the lawn
And look in.
She will watch for you going into the kitchen
And cry, so we let her in.

She eats a lot of mice
But I think she's very nice.
She also eats birds
And she leaves a lot of feathers all over the place!
But I think she's still rather nice.

Emma Hepburn (10)
St Aidan's Primary School

THE TIME MACHINE

T he time machine is ready to fly
H igh up into a colourful sky
E verybody is ready to fly

T o another century
I fly away with a wave and a wink
M y suitcase is packed full of food and drink
E verything's there I hope, I think!

M y pets can all come too!
A nd away we go to 2012
C lever of me to build those shelves
H elping me to unpack my sack
I n my very own time machine
N ew year, new century or even the millennium
E veryone is having fun.

Amy Sloan (10)
St Aidan's Primary School

TRANSPORT

T rains and trucks go very fast, cars and buses too.
R ed narrow boats, police boats too.
A irships are like big hot air balloons and float in the air.
N arrow boats sail very slow on a calm sea.
S ubmarines fire torpedoes under the deep sea.
P eople use transport 24 hours a day.
O range vans and lots of bright colours.
R ed rockets travel high in the dark sky.
T rams travel all over the street on very long tracks.

Marc Montgomery (9)
St Aidan's Primary School

THE TIME MACHINE

T   ime will pass pretty fast
H   urry, come with me
E   veryone thinks it's fun

T   o my time machine we'll go
I   nto the future, away we'll go
M   arvellous sites in the future
E   veryone will have lots of fun

M   ega fun in this year
A   nywhere you go it's clear to see
C   andy mountains! Can you believe it?
H   urry let's go back
I   nto the boring old past
N   ow I know what it is like
E   veryone will love it!

Gemma Fulton (10)
St Aidan's Primary School

SPRING V WINTER

It's Spring in possession with new baby lambs
Passes it to Spring Flower
Who takes it round Snow
Gives it to the roe deer who takes it first time
Straight through Jack Frost in goal
The humans and animals go wild
Substitution by Winter
It's White on the ground
Now it's Green
And there goes the final whistle
Spring is the victor.

Andrew Welsh (11)
St Aidan's Primary School

ADDRESS TO A DOUGHNUT

Of all the cakes in the Sainsbury's range,
You're the one I wouldn't change,
The cookies, buns, tarts and meringues,
All hail your praises in their songs.

You're lovely and round with a hole in the middle,
How you are made is truly a riddle,
Your shape is divine and this I know
Each Friday to Sainsbury's I must go.

Whether sprinkled with sugar or chocolate chips,
You taste delicious on my lips,
Great King of all, that's pure and sweet,
You'll always be my special treat.

Andrew Barton
St Mary's Primary School

LIFE WITHOUT A TATTIE

Breakfast, lunch and dinner, nae tattie,
What wid we dae?
Caviar, salmon, strawberries and cream,
Oh yuck, what muck -
Give me the tattie.

Fried, chipped, boiled or mashed,
A perfect sight, oh what a delight!
White, speckled with brownish skin,
To bake that potato, oh what a sin.

Lashings of butter, tuna and corn,
Mouth-watering, lip-smacking
My tastebuds are taking a whacking.

Tatties wi steak is no mistake,
Tatties wi rice, could never be nice.
Soft and fluffy like eiderdown
Healthy and filling, our jewel in the crown.

Emma Jane McCulloch (9)
St Mary's Primary School

ADDRESS TO SPAGHETTI

Spaghetti, you're the thing I like,
You're big and long and slippery.
And tickly down my throat,
You're messy on my coat.

I like you because you're nice,
I like your lovely smell.
And did you know, you're the best of all.
And when I see you I hear a distant call.

Spaghetti you taste so good to me,
You smell like a *Mediterranean dish.*
I wonder what's for tea tonight?
Spaghetti. Oh I wish!

Rachel McKinnon (8)
St Mary's Primary School

ADDRESS TO A JELLY

Oh poor wee ruby jelly
I see ye sittin' on the shelf and
I cannae help but buy ye 'cause
I know yer guid for my health

I like tae feel yer lovely croon
Yer waist is cool and shiny
An' when I look towards the moon
It minds me o' ye, fair jelly

I always eat ye cool or cauld
I eat ye wi' ice-cream
I like to squeeze ye frae your mauld
Ye come out like a dream

Yer served tae me in a silver tassie
Ye look sae proud an' fine
I need tae keep ye frae the lassies
They say ye taste divine

Ye mean sae much more than food tae me
Ye help me when I'm low
Ye mind me o' the rollin' sea
My frien' my joy my jo.

Kevin Carr (11)
St Mary's Primary School

ADDRESS TO A PIZZA

Aah! Pizza,
You look a tasty treat,
With your toppings nice and neat.
All we do is give you heat,
To make you delicious when I eat.

Toppings that I can change,
Lets me choose how to arrange -
Mushroom tomato, onions and salami.
All good things that will not harm me.
Aah! Pizza you are a joy,
To this certain happy boy.

Santino Palazzo (9)
St Mary's Primary School

UNCLE TAM

I admire some real good poets
Rabbie Burns is one,
But the best poet I ever met,
Is the brother of my mum.

He is my Uncle Thomas,
In the pub he's known as Tam,
And he's the one who inspired me,
To make me the poet I am.

He's one of my four uncles,
Probably the best,
But I'm going to get a doin'
If any of this gets to the rest.

He helped me write my first poem,
I treasure it the most,
And now everyone says I'm brilliant,
But I try not to boast.

He'll probably thank me for this poem,
I'll say, 'Na bother mate,
It's only a little thank you,
For an uncle who is so great.'

David Breakey (11)
St Mary's Primary School

ADDRESS TO A SCOTCH PIE

With smells so good
And crust so brown
With meaty taste
And shape so round.

With rumbling tum
You pass my lips
Served on your own
Or with some chips

Oh great Scotch pie
You taste so good
That's why you are
My favourite food

When you're sizzling
I go crazy
I long to taste you
With some gravy

Burger, hot-dogs they're okay
Great Scotch pie you make
My day.

Sean Gustinelli (9)
St Mary's Primary School

ADDRESS TO A HAZELNUT MERINGUE CAKE

Ye look gid,
Ye feel gid,
Your taste is oot o'u this world.

Ye temp me sae,
A'v git a tingle in ma tae,
When er I think a-boot eating ye.

Ye're broon an' spotty,
A'd call it dotty,
An' your full wi spoons o' sugar.

An your sandwiched the gether wi'
Raspberry and cream,
Och! You're just a dream!

Katie O'Hanlon (11)
St Mary's Primary School

ADDRESS TO MACARONI CHEESE

Macaroni cheese is so yummy
Soft, light and good for the tummy.
Pasta tubes and lots of cheese
Wholesome food, oh yes please!

Macaroni cheese on my spoon
Teatime, supper time or in the afternoon
In the oven or on the plate
Macaroni cheese just smells great!

Cooked in just ten minutes flat
Chef's special, I'm sure of that
Adults, kids, young or old
If on the menu it will be sold!

Pasta here, pasta there
Macaroni cheese is everywhere
In the larder or on the shelf
Ideal with extras or by itself!

Macaroni cheese is dish number one
For the year two thousand and one.
Tastes great, smells great, looks divine
Here ends my little rhyme.

Elisha-Jane Burns (9)
St Mary's Primary School

ADDRESS TO A CADBURY'S CARAMEL

Hard on the outside, soft on the in,
I would not dare put you in the bin.
I love you because you are so delicious,
And to a child very nutritious.
Milky brown chocolate and gold caramel
It's my favourite food, I guess you can tell.

It hits the spot with its scrumptious taste
I know that there won't be any waste.
A melting caramel, chocolate sweet
A delicious, silky, milky treat.
Your aroma is simply divine,
You yummy, tasty sweet, of course you'll be mine.

You tempt me when I see you in the shop
Once I start eating you, I canny stop
I unwrap the foil and gobble you up,
Until the eight pieces are gone . . . that's my lot.
Soft golden caramel trickling out,
This bar of chocolate I can't do without.

Jenna Kelly (11)
St Mary's Primary School

SPAGHETTI BOLOGNESE

Spaghetti Bolognese is a meal I adore
and when my mum makes it I always want more
It is made from pasta, tomatoes and mince
after first trying it, I have loved it since

The reason I enjoy this wonderful meal
I suppose is because of the pasta I feel
wriggling up the spoon, the fork and then past my lips
after passing the tomatoes and mince in which it dips

It is usually eaten with a fork and a spoon
and the aroma that comes from it can fill the room
We usually have it around dinner time
and the more that I'm given suits me just fine

I am often tempted to eat the full lot
of the contents that mum has put in the pot
Then mum has to warn me, I could make myself sick
so I satisfy myself and give my plate a last *lick!*

Laura Jones (11)
St Mary's Primary School

VOLCANIC DEVASTATION

Thick black smoke covering the sky
As an avalanche of lava spurts out.
Destroying everything in its way,
Households and towns underground!

People fleeing for their lives
As the burning lava covers the ground.
Children crying, people dying
Because of the destruction all around!

As the lava turns to rock
Redevelopment goes ahead.
This little town may be safe for now
But no one can predict the future!

David Duffy (11)
St Monica's Primary School

VOLCANO

As the spurting flames
Exploded into the open
Thick black smoke
Covered the sky
Only a trickle of sunlight
Pushing through.
When the disaster disappeared,
The screaming people reappeared
All the sweating and the bleeding
They had done to make
Their village appear again.

Gareth Docherty (11)
St Monica's Primary School

MORNING SOUNDS

Ring, ring, the alarm clock goes,
Clinking clink, cups clatter.
Sizzle, sizzle the sausages fry,
Bang, bang the door batters.
Splash, splash the water splashes,
Slam, slam out the door, Dad dashes!

Debbie Hamill (9)
St Monica's Primary School

THE WRATH OF THE VOLCANO

A volcano
Like a raging mountain
Spurts out
Like a fountain.

With its fiery breath
And its fearsome wrath
Destroys all that cross
Its path.

Barbara Anne Hogg (11)
St Monica's Primary School

WHAT'S THAT?

Clink, clink, in the night
I heard a creak and I got a fright.
'What's that?' I said to myself
'Maybe it's a monster or an elf.'

Then I heard someone knocking on the door
I stood up and it fell to the floor.
I went over to see what was there,
It was my little sister's teddy bear!

Stephen McSwiggan (9)
St Monica's Primary School

VOLCANO

I see the black smoke
I hear the lava's rage
This time I'll stay away
Don't look, walk or run
The lava is coming near
They're all melting.
What should we do?
Just run away
The volcano is here.

David Cameron (11)
St Monica's Primary School

VOLCANO

A mountain of lava
Erupting furiously,
Thick black smoke
Swooping everywhere.

Widespread destruction
Taking over the town
Darkened skies
Blocking the sun.

Molten lava, leaping flames
Like a red-hot river,
People running
Homes lost, villages ruined.
No more sound!

Reborn villages, homes and towns,
Rich lush pastures on the ground.
Planting seeds all over again
We have our village back!

Louise Docherty (11)
St Monica's Primary School

ICE CREAM

Ice cream cold and yummy,
Chocolate sauce and gleaming ice.
Eating ice cream seems such fun,
Cream so silk and white.

Running cream, coming down the cone,
Eating cone is so crispy,
At the end, just one more bit . . .
More ice cream will make me sick!

Samantha Craw (9)
St Monica's Primary School

VOLCANO

The sky is blackened
By the smoke
Red hot lava
Lost towns and cities
People running
Others engulfed
In a red-hot river.

Ashleigh McKenna (11)
St Monica's Primary School

LAVA

Lava spurting
Swamping everything
Thick black smoke
Covers the sky.
People run for their lives
Screaming, shouting.
Nothing can save them.

Kieran Rafferty (11)
St Monica's Primary School

BONNIE BEN

It all started just over two years
I was so desperate for a puppy
I was brought to tears.
Then one day mum finally agreed,
And along you came
With her little breed.

You were so nice and very cute,
Who knew you'd turn into
A little brute.
Mum couldn't handle you any more,
You had six weeks to behave
Or you'd be out the door.

You didn't make it, my little friend,
Mum cried 'He's out
This is the end!'
You were going, we didn't know where
But along came grandad and said
'Don't you dare!
You can't toss wee Ben out to be all alone,
Give him to me and I'll take him home.'

Now you're happy when you go for a walk,
Grandad is even teaching you to talk.
I know I love you, my little pup,
Even though you're young
And still growing up.

Nadine O'Byrne (8)
St Monica's Primary School

DEVASTATION

Ash rain
Spurting into the sky
Thousands of people die!
An avalanche of molten lava,
Wiping everything
In its path.

A mushroom cloud
Thick black smoke,
Homes collapsing
People running for their lives,
As the lava flow ends
Silence in the town.

Kieran Starrs (11)
St Monica's Primary School

VOLCANIC DESTRUCTION

Volcano erupting
Molten lava spurting
Thick black smoke
People screaming
A chilling feeling
Everything shaking
Everything burning
A thick liquid
Red lava
Leaping flames
Dark skies above our heads.

Ryan Pryce (11)
St Monica's Primary School

VOLCANO CHAOS

Raining fire
A cover of ash
Blocking the sun
What chaos.
As I watch helplessly
Oh, the horror
Of people on fire
Villages wiped out
Houses destroyed.

Daniel Duffy (11)
St Monica's Primary School

COLOURS

Red is the sky before I go to bed
Red is blood dripping from my knee.
Yellow is the sun on a hot summer's day
Yellow is butter melting on your toast
Blue is a clear sky when there's no clouds in sight
Blue is the sea on a calm dry day
Green is the grass swaying back and forth
Green is the Christmas tree at the window of my house
Black is a witch flying through the sky
Black is long straight hair
White is a whiteboard in my classroom
White is chalk on a classroom blackboard
Orange is a juicy orange
Orange is fresh juice that people in the early morning drink.

Suzy Kennedy (10)
St Patrick's Primary School

BEDTIME

Bedtime for me
I can see
The wax in my lava lamp
Bouncing up . . . and down

Bedtime for me
I can hear
Cars zooming past
So very fast

Bedtime for me
I can taste
The blue minty paste
Stuck onto my tongue

Bedtime for me
I can touch
The long, soft, feathery pillow
With my head in the middle of it

Bedtime for me
I can smell
The fruity shampoo
Dancing about on my head

Bedtime for me
Time to sleep
Feeling lonely and tired
I pull up the covers and close my eyes

Jenna Nelson (10)
St Patrick's Primary School

COLOURS

I like the colour red, it reminds me of Christmas
Red is Santa's suit or red are peoples' noses on
Red Nose day, or even red is strawberries.

I hate the colour black it reminds me of dark
creepy nights and old rusty witches.

I love the colour gold, it reminds me of angel's wings
and my golden hair.

I don't really like the colour white, it reminds
me of ghosts and it's really plain against other colours.

I love the colour yellow, it reminds me of
sunny Spain and the hot sunshine.

I like the colour silver, it reminds me of
the lovely ocean and the stars reflecting on the sea.

I love the colour blue, it reminds me of summer nights
and the funny story of the blue elephant.

I like the colour orange it reminds me of an orange ball
and the summer.

Natalie Duffy (10)
St Patrick's Primary School

MOODS

Sometimes when I go to my grans
I think it's marvellous
When I play with her dog Bonny
I love walking her
We play fetch.

Sometimes my mum says to me
You can't go outside
Because it's too cold
And I make a face behind her back!

Louise McAnna (9)
St Patrick's Primary School

COLOURS

White is a ghost glowing in the dark
White is a paper coming from a packet.

Green is the grass in summer
Green is a Christmas tree at Christmas.

Red is danger - a sign of death
Red is a fire burning down.

Blue is the sky with no clouds
Blue is the sea glistening.

Black is the sky at 10 o'clock in the winter
Black is as black as the ground - just been tarred.

Orange is an orange - just been bought.
Orange is the sun setting.

Yellow is a banana skin
Yellow is the sun shining.

Silver is wrapping paper on special gifts.
Silver is the moon shining at night.

Stefan Ross (10)
St Patrick's Primary School

MY MUM AND DAD

My mum

As beautiful as a red rose,
As kind as can be
And cool like me!
If she ever dies and forgets my name
I will love her just the same.

My dad

As bossy as my head teacher
As kind as my gran and granda
He is obsessed with football!
And won't talk to me at all
He will always love Celtic as long as he lives
But I will always love him as long as I live.

Paul Milloy (9)
St Patrick's Primary School

THRESHOLD OF SPACE

I look back and see
the big green tree
and the friends that played with me.
I look forward and wonder
how the houses will look.
Do we drive or fly
to where the school will be?
I wonder what the future will hold for me.

David Wright (11)
St Patrick's Primary School

SUMMER

Barefoot on the beach.
I like to feel warm
Soggy sand covering my feet.
Hot summer's days
In my back garden.
Barefoot on the beach
I hate to feel crabs
Grabbing my feet.
It makes me feel
Uncomfortable
And angry!
It reminds me
Of a bee sting
When I was in a pet shop
When I was six years old.

Amy Jennifer Waugh (9)
St Patrick's Primary School

THRESHOLD OF SPACE

I look back and see the Earth
and wonder what's going on?
The Earth looks so small
like the size of a ball.

I look forward and wonder
what lies out there?
More people like us,
Or aliens with no hair.

Catherine Milloy (11)
St Patrick's Primary School

MOODS

Sometimes I'm in a talkative mood
Because my big sister and I keep talking
And my big brother says to us
'Put a sock in it!'
Sometimes I'm in a happy mood
Because I fall back in with Linzi.
Then we go swimming or play outside.
Sometimes I'm in a moody mood
Because my mum says that
I can't go swimming.
Then she says 'What's wrong with you?
You can't get everything you want, you know!'

Gennifer Bennett (8)
St Patrick's Primary School

MY DAD

My daddy's hair is as bright as the sun
As spiky as a hedgehog
He is 29 years old,
His eyes are dark brown
With glasses like cuboids.
He wears joggy bottoms and a T-shirt
And he makes me laugh.
But the thing I like most
Is that I love him
And he loves me.

Carly Mooney (9)
St Patrick's Primary School

THRESHOLD OF SPACE

I look back and see a
worn out planet called Earth.
With not many inhabitants
and a shallow envelope of air.

I look forward and wonder
what will the future be like?
Who will we meet?
What will we find?
What other galaxies will we discover?
In the threshold of space.

Charlotte Boyle (10)
St Patrick's Primary School

TRAVELLERS IN SPACE

Look back and see the big blue Earth
The clouds and land
It looks like a pearl

I look forward and wonder
What will it be like
Will they like me?
Will I like them?

Evan Duffy (11)
St Patrick's Primary School

MY GRAN

My gran is as sweet as a rose from the ground
My gran smells of perfume
My gran is as cuddly as a bunny
My gran is beautiful like a teddy
My gran has lovely silver glasses.

Donna McKendrick (9)
St Patrick's Primary School

MY COUSIN

My cousin is as daft as a clown
And his hair is as golden as the sun.
The way that he laughs is funny
And he is the most annoying person in the world
I'm glad he's mine!

Colleen Murphy (9)
St Patrick's Primary School

MY GRAN

She has soft curly hair
She smells like a rose.
She is as sweet as a bunny
Her eyes are as blue as the sky.
She looks like a teddy!

Kelly Jarvis (9)
St Patrick's Primary School

BAREFOOT ON THE BEACH

Barefoot on the beach.
I like to feel the warm water on my feet,
It makes me feel warm and nice.
It reminds me of a beautiful hot summer's day.

I hate to feel the slimy seaweed curl
round my feet.
It makes me feel sick.
It reminds me of ugly fish
Circling round my feet.

Erin Kane (9)
St Patrick's Primary School

BAREFOOT ON THE BEACH

Barefoot on the beach.
I like to feel the soft, warm sand
It reminds me of stepping on the ground
When it's been hot.

Barefoot on the beach.
I hate when I step on sharp stones or rocks.
It reminds me of stepping on very rough ground.
It makes me feel bad.

Danielle Marshall (9)
St Patrick's Primary School

MY FAMILY

My mum smells like roses
She is a big bundle of posies.
My dad is like a frog
He loves to jog.
My brother is as bossy as a bee
But he is a good friend to me.

Dana McMahon (8)
St Patrick's Primary School

MY MUM

My mum has short, brown hair
She is always working.
She is the best mum ever
And she never forgets about me
She is as pretty as a beautiful butterfly.

Linda Wright (9)
St Patrick's Primary School

MY BROTHER

As ugly as a monster
As bossy as a bee
As funny as a comedian
But not as funny as me!

Samantha Innes (9)
St Patrick's Primary School

BAREFOOT ON THE BEACH

Barefoot on the beach.
I like to feel the very hot sand
in-between my feet.
It makes me feel hot and happy.
It reminds me of hot summer's days.

Barefoot on the beach.
I hate to feel a very jaggy crab,
It makes me feel very stingy.
It reminds me of being stung by
a jaggy nettle.

Christopher Dale (9)
St Patrick's Primary School

BAREFOOT ON THE BEACH

Barefoot on the beach.
I like to feel the squidgy sand
On the bottom of my feet.
It makes me feel comfy and relaxed.

Barefoot on the beach.
I hate to feel the slimy jellyfish
On the soles of my feet,
It makes me feel very scared.

Lauren Neilson (9)
St Patrick's Primary School

COLOURS

Red is a *danger* sign warning you to *stop*
Red is dark *blood* oozing out of a very large wound.

Orange is a *flaring fire* smouldering at a house
Orange is the *sun* beaming down on us all.

Green is my hoops *Celtic top* on my body when I'm
cheering for my team.
Green is the grass cut nice and straight and short.

White is my writing paper sitting in front of me
White is a fluffy cloud in the sky turning into different shapes.

Blue is my eyes, the same colour as most of my friends
Blue is the river flowing along, fast and slow.

Yellow is my Record of Achievement, sitting on the shelf
Yellow is Stefan's hair, short and dark at the back.

Gold is a new door handle being screwed onto the door,
Gold is a new ring being placed on my finger.

Silver is my mum's Rennie Macintosh earrings dangle from her ears
Silver is the moon and the stars resting in the clear dark sky.

Black is the sky at night, sometimes foggy, sometimes alive with stars
Black is when my light gets switched off at night, dark, safe, comfy,
then I go to sleep.

Lauren Hughes (10)
St Patrick's Primary School

COLOURS

Gold is the colour of Tutankhamun's death mask shining in the sun
Gold is the sun flickering at dawn

Silver is a diamond, dazzling in a Queen's crown
Silver is a gel pen colouring in my picture

Black is a dark room with the moon beaming through
Black are my trousers gleaming on my body

Blue is a football team when they go out on the field
Blue is the sky when I look up

Green is a football team when they win the Premier Cup
Green is my sweatshirt when it sees a beam of light

Orange is an orange rolling down a hill
Orange is the end of the tricolour flag

Red is my friends' faces when they laugh with joy
Red is a hot tomato when it bursts from its seed

White is a piece of icing sugar melted on a cake
White is a shaggy Scottish terrier running for its bone

Yellow is the sun beaming out with light
Yellow is a banana squashed like a pancake.

Alisdair McCann (10)
St Patrick's Primary School